C000273197

Susannah Reed

Super Minds

Teacher's Resource Book Starter

CAMBRIDGE
UNIVERSITY PRESS

CAMBRIDGE
UNIVERSITY PRESS

University Printing House, Cambridge CB2 8BS, United Kingdom

One Liberty Plaza, 20th Floor, New York, NY 10006, USA

477 Williamstown Road, Port Melbourne, VIC 3207, Australia

314-321, 3rd Floor, Plot 3, Splendor Forum, Jasola District Centre, New Delhi - 110025, India

79 Anson Road, #06-04/06, Singapore 079906

Cambridge University Press is part of the University of Cambridge.

It furthers the University's mission by disseminating knowledge in the pursuit of education, learning and research at the highest international levels of excellence.

www.cambridge.org
Information on this title: www.cambridge.org/9781107640139

© Cambridge University Press 2012

This publication is in copyright. Subject to statutory exception and to the provisions of relevant collective licensing agreements, no reproduction of any part may take place without the written permission of Cambridge University Press.

First published 2012
Reprinted 2019

A catalogue record for this publication is available from the British Library

ISBN 978-1-107-64013-9 Teacher's Resource Book Starter
ISBN 978-0-521-14852-8 Student's Book with DVD-ROM Starter
ISBN 978-0-521-14853-5 Workbook Starter
ISBN 978-0-521-21433-9 Teacher's Book Starter
ISBN 978-0-521-21434-6 Class Audio CDs Starter
ISBN 978-0-521-22163-4 Flashcards Starter
ISBN 978-0-521-14854-2 Classware and Interactive DVD-ROM Starter

Cambridge University Press has no responsibility for the persistence or accuracy of URLs for external or third-party internet websites referred to in this publication, and does not guarantee that any content on such websites is, or will remain, accurate or appropriate. Information regarding prices, travel timetables, and other factual information given in this work is correct at the time of first printing but Cambridge University Press does not guarantee the accuracy of such information thereafter.

Contents

Introduction

What does the Teacher's Resource Book provide?

The Teacher's Resource Book provides additional photocopiable worksheets for those students following the *Super Minds* Starter level. Each worksheet has accompanying teacher's notes with suggestions for exploitation in the classroom, together with suggested optional follow-up activities.

The worksheets have been carefully designed to reinforce and provide extra practice of the work done in class. They focus on the language introduced in the Starter level of the course and do not introduce or use any additional or unfamiliar language. There are four worksheets provided for each main unit in the Starter level:

Worksheet 1: This worksheet focuses on the key vocabulary presented on the opening page of each unit in the Student's Book. The vocabulary is listed at the foot of the worksheet.

Worksheet 2: This worksheet focuses on the language presented and practised in the first grammar lesson of each unit (on the second page of the unit in the Student's Book). The target language is at the foot of the worksheet.

Worksheet 3: This worksheet focuses on the language presented and practised in the second grammar lesson of each unit (on the fourth page of the unit in the Student's Book). Once again, the target language is at the foot of the worksheet.

Worksheet 4: This worksheet is based on the CLIL content of each unit (on pages seven and eight in each unit of the Student's Book).

In addition, there are three worksheets provided for use with the Hello unit.

How can the worksheets be used?

The worksheets can be used in a number of ways:

- **The first three worksheets in each unit** have been designed so that students can work on them either individually or as part of pair or class activities. For individual work, the worksheets can be used for those students who finish class activities more quickly than others. For pair or class activities, the worksheets can be used when additional practice is necessary, for revision, for an alternative activity when there is a gap or change in your usual lesson planning routine or they can be set for homework. Suggestions for how to use the worksheets in the different ways are included in the accompanying teacher's notes.

- **The fourth worksheet in each unit** (the CLIL worksheet) is intended to be used communicatively, for pair, small group or class activities. These worksheets include games and craft activities. Suggestions for how to use these worksheets are also included in the accompanying teacher's notes.

What activity types do the worksheets provide?

The worksheets provide a range of fun pre-reading puzzles and activities, including matching puzzles, colouring puzzles, spot the difference, jigsaw activities, matching pairs, odd one out and other observation activities. There are also board games and games such as Bingo. All activities are designed to be used without an audio accompaniment.

Most of the worksheets are wordless. However, from Unit 5, some simple word labels of the key vocabulary items are included, where appropriate, on the first worksheet for each unit. This mirrors the introduction to text labels in the Workbook and is intended for text recognition only rather than for true reading.

The teacher's notes and optional follow-up activities contain references to some well-known traditional games and activities. These include:

Snap! Students play in pairs or small groups. They will need several sets of picture cards which they shuffle and deal out between them. They take turns to place a card from their pack face up on the table in front of them. If their card matches the one their partner has placed on the table, they call out *Snap!* The first one to do so wins the pile of cards. The game continues until one student has all the cards and is the winner.

Simon says! Call out instructions for students to follow. If you say the instruction with *Simon says* at the beginning of it, e.g. *Simon says, 'Stand up'*, they should do as you say. Without the instruction *Simon says* at the beginning, e.g. *Stand up*, students should do nothing. If they follow an instruction wrongly, they are 'out' and have to sit down. They can also play this game in small groups.

Matching pairs Students play this game in pairs or small groups. They lay out sets of cards face down on a table then take turns to turn up two cards at a time, one from each set, and name them. If the two cards match, they keep them. If they don't, they replace the cards in the same place on the table. As the game continues, students remember where the cards are and start matching pairs from memory. The winner is the student who has the most matching pairs at the end of the game.

Hopscotch Chalk a Hopscotch grid onto the floor or playground (see page 29). Students play in pairs. Each has a stone. The first player tries to throw their stone exactly onto the square marked 1. If it lands correctly, he or she hops over square 1 and lands on squares 2 and 3 with one foot totally inside each square. They continue up the grid, hopping onto square 4 with one foot then squares 5 and 6 with two feet and so on until square 10 where they turn around and move back down the grid in the same way. Stopping at squares 2 and 3, they pick up their stone from square 1. If they complete this without any mistakes, they then throw their stone onto square 2 and repeat the process, this time missing out square 2. If they make any mistakes, it is the other player's turn. Players continue where they left off until one player has thrown their stone correctly onto all ten squares.

Noughts and crosses Students play with a grid of nine squares containing different pictures (see page 48). One student is *noughts* (0) and the other is *crosses* (X). One student starts by choosing a picture on the grid and making a sentence about it. If the sentence is correct, they draw their nought (or cross) in the box provided next to the picture. If the sentence is incorrect, they draw nothing. Their partner then has a turn. The game continues until one student has drawn three noughts or crosses in a vertical, horizontal or diagonal line. This student is the winner.

Bingo Students choose and circle three or four pictures from a vocabulary group. Call out words or sentences about the pictures. Students listen. When they hear you call out a word or sentence about a picture they have chosen, they cross it out. The first one to put a cross on all the pictures they have chosen calls out *Bingo!*

Spinners As an alternative to using dice in board games, students can make and use a spinner. The spinner is made by drawing a circle and then dividing it into six equal segments by drawing lines. Students should then cut off the 'arc' of each segment on the outside of the circle so that there is a straight edge going across the widest part of each segment. They then write the numbers from one to six, one in each segment. Finally, a hole is made in the centre of the circle and a pencil pushed through. Students can then spin the pencil with their thumb and first two fingers. The number it rests on each time is used to play the game.

Worksheet 1: Hello, Gina!

Using the worksheet

- This matching activity practises *Hello* and the names of the main characters from the course *Mike, Polly, Leo* and *Gina*.

- Students say the names of the characters they can see at the top of the worksheet. They then find the same characters hiding in the jungle and draw lines to match them up.

- Students can then work in pairs, saying *Hello* and the name of a character, e.g. *Hello, Gina!*, for their partner to find and point to in the jungle.

Optional follow-up activity: Students play a mime game, in pairs or small groups. They take turns to choose a character and mime them. The others guess who they are and say, e.g. *Hello, Mike*.

Worksheet 2: Hello! What's your name?

Using the worksheet

- This craft activity practises *Hello! What's your name? I'm …*

- Students work in groups of four. They each choose which puppet they want to make, then cut it out and colour it in. They make the puppets' legs by putting their fingers through the holes from behind. Help as necessary.

- Students can then use the puppets to practise asking and answering, e.g. *Hello! What's your name? I'm Gina*.

Optional follow-up activity: Students play a matching game. Play some music and ask students to circulate around the class, with their puppets hidden behind their back. When the music stops, students say to the person nearest to them *Hello! What's your name?* That person holds up their puppet and replies, e.g. *I'm Gina*. Students have to find as many in the class as they can who have the same puppet as them. At the end of the activity, all the *Ginas, Mikes, Leos* and *Pollys* can stand together.

Worksheet 3: Colours

Using the worksheet

- This colouring activity practises the colours *red, yellow, blue, green, purple* and *orange*.

- Students work alone and colour the sections in the top caterpillar in a sequence of colours of their choice.

- Students then work in pairs to do a colour dictation activity. Without looking at their partner's picture, they take it in turns to dictate their colour sequence, starting at the head, to their partner, who listens and colours in the bottom caterpillar accordingly.

- They then compare their pictures.

Optional follow-up activity: Students play a colour race in the classroom. Divide the class into six groups and allocate each one a colour. Set a time limit for them to find as many objects as they can in that colour. The group with the most objects is the winner. You can teach them the English words for some of these objects if you wish, but the colour words should be the focus of this activity.

Worksheet 1: Hello, Gina!

Say the names. Find the animals.

Vocabulary: Mike, Polly, Leo, Gina

PHOTOCOPIABLE © Cambridge University Press 2012   *Super Minds* Teacher's Resource Book Starter

Worksheet 2: Hello!
What's your name?

Make finger puppets. Then ask and answer.

Grammar: Hello! What's your name? I'm ...

Super Minds Teacher's Resource Book Starter   © Cambridge University Press 2012   **PHOTOCOPIABLE**

Worksheet 3: Colours

Colour. Then say, listen and colour.

Colours: red, blue, green, orange, purple, yellow

PHOTOCOPIABLE © Cambridge University Press 2012   *Super Minds* Teacher's Resource Book Starter

1 My classroom

Worksheet 1: My classroom things

Using the worksheet

- This drawing activity practises vocabulary for things in the classroom *pencil, chair, bag, rubber, book, desk*.

- Students match the pictures of the classroom objects to the dotted outline pictures of the same objects. They then trace round the dotted outline pictures and add any other details to make the pairs of pictures match completely.

- They can then work in pairs. One student says the name of an object and their partner points to the object in the pictures.

KEY: 2c, 3d, 4f, 5a, 6b

Optional follow-up activity: Students find and point to the different items in the classroom. Using the smaller items, e.g. *pen, rubber,* or using flashcards, you can also play a guessing game. Hide an object or flashcard behind your back and ask students to guess what it is, by calling out, e.g. *pen.* Those students who guess correctly can then have a turn at hiding an object.

Worksheet 2: Stand up. Sit down.

Using the worksheet

- This colouring activity practises classroom instructions *Sit down, Stand up, Open (your book), Close (your book), Pick up (a rubber / a pencil), Put (your bag / your book on the desk)*.

- Students find matching pairs and colour their T-shirts in their unique colours, as in the example. They say the action in the picture each time. Students can either do this individually or in pairs. If working in pairs, one student says an instruction, e.g. *Pick up a rubber,* and their partner has to listen and find the two pictures and colour them.

KEY: b and p Open your book. c and i Close your book. d and m Pick up a pencil. e and o Put your book on the desk. g and j Sit down. h and k Put your bag on the desk. l and n Pick up a rubber.

Optional follow-up activity: These pictures can also be cut up and made into a set of cards. Students can combine their sets of cards to play a game of *Snap!* (see page 4), in pairs or small groups.

Worksheet 3: Numbers 1 to 6

Using the worksheet

- This counting activity practises numbers 1 to 6 and revises classroom objects *pencil, bag, chair, desk, rubber, book*.

- Students look at the example. A second chair has been drawn to match the number on the domino. Students look at each domino and say the number. They then count the objects and draw additional objects as necessary to make the pictures match the number.

- They can then play a counting game in pairs. Students take turns to hold up a number of fingers for their partner to point to the correct domino and say what they see, e.g. *four books.*

Optional follow-up activity: Play a game of *Guess the number* with the class. Trace a number in the air with your finger. Students look and hold up the correct number of fingers. Choose one student to say the number. Students can also play this game in pairs, by tracing a number on their partner's back for them to guess.

Worksheet 4: Actions at school

Using the worksheet

- This board game revises classroom action verbs *read, write, sing, count, draw, sit down, stand up, open/close (your book), pick up (a pencil)*.

- Students play the game in pairs or small groups. They will need counters, dice or spinners (see page 5) and a different colour pen each.

- Students put their counters on the board next to the Start arrow. They take it in turns to throw the dice or spin the spinner and move around the board. When they land on an action, they must give the command for their partner to act out. If they say it correctly, they can put a coloured mark next to it on the board. Students continue travelling round the board until one of them has marked all the actions in their colour. Alternatively, set a time limit. The student who has marked the most actions at the end of this time limit is the winner.

Optional follow-up activity: Play a game of *Simon says!* using the actions from the worksheet (see page 4).

Worksheet 1: My classroom things

Match and draw.

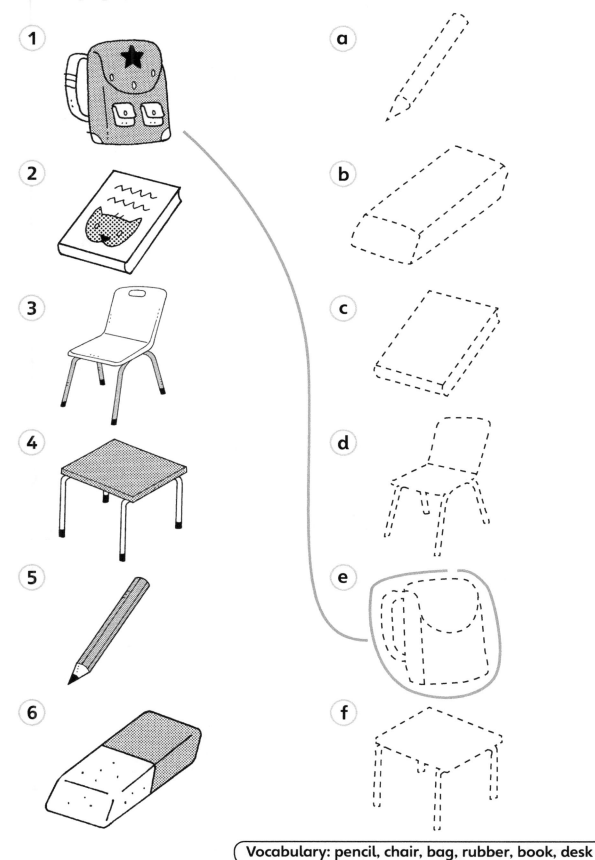

Vocabulary: pencil, chair, bag, rubber, book, desk

PHOTOCOPIABLE © Cambridge University Press 2012   *Super Minds* Teacher's Resource Book Starter

Worksheet 2: Stand up. Sit down.

Find, match and colour.

Grammar 1: Stand up. Sit down. Open … Close … Pick up … Put …

Super Minds Teacher's Resource Book Starter   © Cambridge University Press 2012   **PHOTOCOPIABLE**

① Worksheet 3: Numbers 1 to 6

Look and say. Then count and draw.

Grammar 2: one, two, three, four, five, six

© Cambridge University Press 2012   *Super Minds* Teacher's Resource Book Starter

PHOTOCOPIABLE

Play the game. Say and do!

Actions at school

② My family

Worksheet 1: People in my family

Using the worksheet

- This matching activity practises family vocabulary *mum*, *dad*, *brother*, *sister*, *grandma*, *grandpa*.

- Students match the silhouettes to the correct family members in the photo by drawing a line. They then say the words for the family members. Students can work individually or in pairs.

KEY: 2d, 3c, 4f, 5a, 6e

Optional follow-up activity: Students play a guessing game in pairs. One chooses a family member and copies their position and facial expression from the picture. Their partner has to look and guess who they are by saying either e.g. *the brother* or *brother*.

Worksheet 2: This is my brother.

Using the worksheet

- This jigsaw activity practises the structure *This is my …* and family vocabulary *sister*, *dad*, *mum*, *grandpa*.

- Students cut out the parts of each picture and place or stick them on a sheet of paper to create the four hidden family members. They can then describe them to a partner as if they are the boy monster in the top corner, using the first person: *This is my sister*, etc.

KEY: **1** This is my sister. **2** This is my dad. **3** This is my mum. **4** This is my grandpa.

Optional follow-up activity: Students make their own puzzle pictures. They draw a picture of one of the monster's family members and then cut this into pieces for their partner to put back into order and name: *This is my grandma*, etc.

Worksheet 3: This is my pencil.

Using the worksheet

- This observation activity practises the structure *This is my …* and revises classroom objects *bag*, *pencil*, *rubber*, *book*, *desk*, *chair*.

- Students note the object each child is holding or interacting with and then find and circle it in the row of objects next to each picture. They should say e.g. *This is my (book)* as they find and circle the object each time. Students can work individually or in pairs.

KEY: **2a** This is my chair. **3b** This is my rubber. **4c** This is my pencil. **5a** This is my desk. **6c** This is my bag.

Optional follow-up activity: Students play a simple *Say and find* activity in pairs. They put their possessions on the desk. One student describes one of their possessions, e.g. *This is my book*. Their partner listens and points to the correct object.

Worksheet 4: Families

Using the worksheet

- This board game revises the structure *This is my …* and family vocabulary *sister*, *brother*, *mum*, *dad*, *grandma*, *grandpa*.

- Students play the game in pairs. They will need a dice or spinner (see page 5) and counters.

- Students each choose a family card, place their counters on the Start square and then take turns to throw the dice and travel round the board, collecting the different members of that family. When they land on a square with a member of the family they are collecting, they say e.g. *This is my (dad)* and tick off that family member on their card. When they land on a member of their partner's family, or one they have already ticked, or a blank square, they do nothing. They carry on travelling round the board in a circle until one student has collected all the members of their family. This student is the winner.

Optional follow-up activity: Students cut out (and colour in) the family members on their 'family' cards and then combine them with those of another pair to play a game of Matching pairs (see page 4).

② Worksheet 1: People in my family

Find and match. Then say.

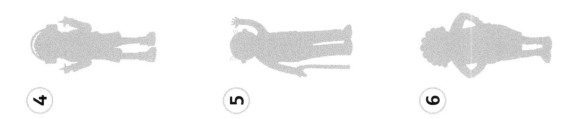

Vocabulary: grandpa, grandma, mum, dad, sister, brother

Super Minds Teacher's Resource Book Starter © Cambridge University Press 2012 **PHOTOCOPIABLE**

2 Worksheet 2: This is my brother.

Make and say.

Grammar 1: This is my (brother).

PHOTOCOPIABLE © Cambridge University Press 2012   *Super Minds* Teacher's Resource Book Starter   17

Look and circle. Then say.

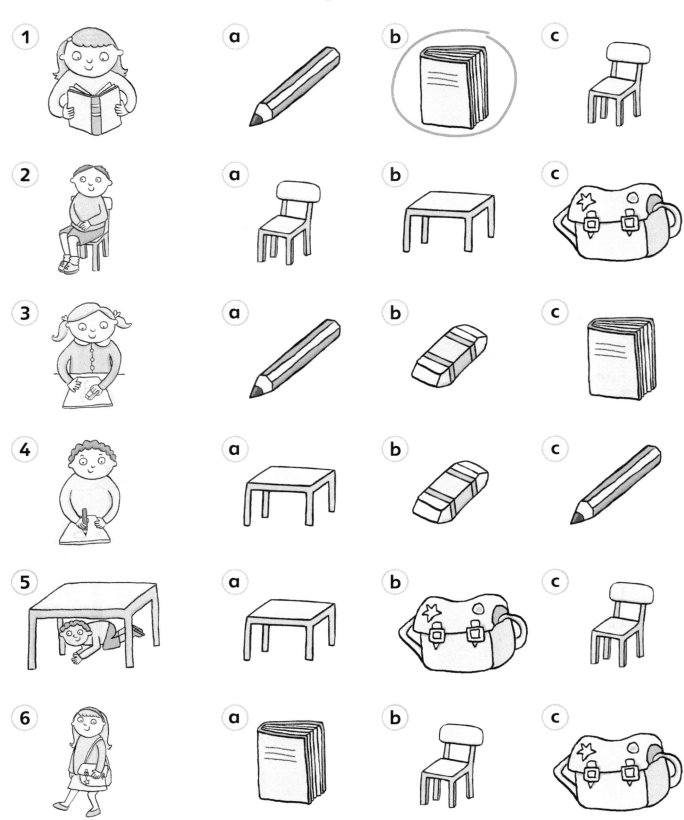

Grammar 2: This is my (pencil).

Worksheet 4: Families

Play the game.

Family 1

Family 2

Start ➡️

Families

PHOTOCOPIABLE © Cambridge University Press 2012   *Super Minds* Teacher's Resource Book Starter   19

③ My face

Worksheet 1: My face

Using the worksheet

- This cut out and stick activity practises vocabulary for facial features *eyes, ears, nose, face, teeth, mouth*.

- Students cut out and match the facial features to the correct face. They then stick them into place, saying the name of each facial feature as they do so.

- This can also be done in pairs. Students take a face each. They cut out the facial features and place them on the table. They then take turns to say a facial feature. Their partner has to choose the appropriate picture and give it to them to stick on their picture.

Optional follow-up activity: Students play a game of *Mirror, mirror* in pairs. They sit opposite each other and say one of the six 'face' words. Their partner has to touch or move that part of their face. The speaker has to try and copy their movement at the same time as they are doing it.

Worksheet 2: I'm angry.

Using the worksheet

- This jigsaw activity practises the structure *I'm …* and the emotions *happy, angry, sad, scared*.

- Students look at the pictures of the children and try to guess what their emotions are by the expressions in their eyes. They then find the missing mouth for each child and match these to the correct pictures by drawing lines.

- Encourage students to make each expression and say e.g. *I'm sad* as they match the puzzle pieces.

KEY: 2c I'm scared. 3d I'm angry. 4a I'm happy.

Optional follow-up activity: Play a game of *Mixed-up emotions*. The worksheet activity will have encouraged students to see how we express emotions with our eyes and our mouths. Ask students to try and make faces which combine different emotions in their eyes and mouths, e.g. *happy eyes and sad mouths*. Students try to make a happy expression in their eyes while making a sad expression with their mouths. They will probably find this both difficult and amusing. Students can then play in pairs, combining two emotions for their partner to guess, e.g. *You're angry and sad!*

Worksheet 3: Are you angry?

Using the worksheet

- This odd one out activity practises the structures *Are you … ? Yes, I am / No, I'm not* and revises vocabulary for emotions *angry, happy, sad, scared*.

- Students find the face in each row that is showing a different emotion from the others and circle it. They say the emotions they can see each time.

- Students can then use the pictures to play a guessing game in pairs. They take turns to secretly choose one of the monsters on the page. Their partner has to guess who they are by asking, e.g. *Are you in number 1? (Yes, I am.) Are you angry? (No, I'm not.) Are you sad? (Yes, I am.)*

KEY: 2a, 3b, 4d

Optional follow-up activity: Students play the 'odd one out' game in class. Ask four volunteers to come to the front of the class. Secretly ask three of them to mime one emotion, e.g. *sad*, and the fourth to mime another, e.g. *scared*. Students try to guess the odd one out and check by asking the volunteers in turn, e.g. *Are you scared?* Volunteers answer *Yes, I am. / No, I'm not.*

Worksheet 4: Music and feelings

Using the worksheet

- This activity practises musical instrument vocabulary *violin, drum, recorder* and *xylophone* and revises emotions *sad, angry, happy, scared*.

- Students each cut out the eight cards. They then combine them with those of a partner in two piles: one with instruments and one with emotions.

- They shuffle the cards in each pile. Then, together, they turn over the top card on each pile and say the words for what they see, e.g. *happy, drum*, putting the cards to one side if they are sure of the words and replacing them in the pile if they are not.

- When they are sure of all the words, they replace the cards in the appropriate piles. They take turns to secretly turn over a card from each pile and do a mime that combines the instrument and the emotion shown, e.g. playing the violin in a very happy or angry way. Their partner has to say the words that relate to the mime, e.g. *violin, angry*. If they are right, their partner then has a turn.

Optional follow-up activity: Bring pieces of music to class and play them to students. They listen and say whether the music makes them feel happy, angry, sad or scared.

③ Worksheet 1: My face

Match and stick. Then say.

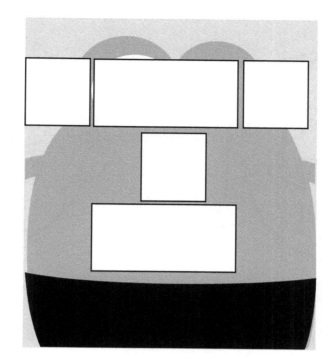

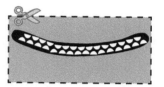

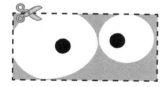

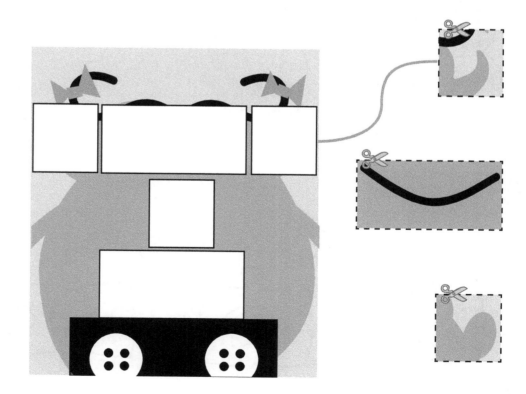

Vocabulary: eyes, ears, nose, face, teeth, mouth

PHOTOCOPIABLE © Cambridge University Press 2012   *Super Minds* Teacher's Resource Book Starter

Worksheet 2: I'm angry.

Find and match. Then say.

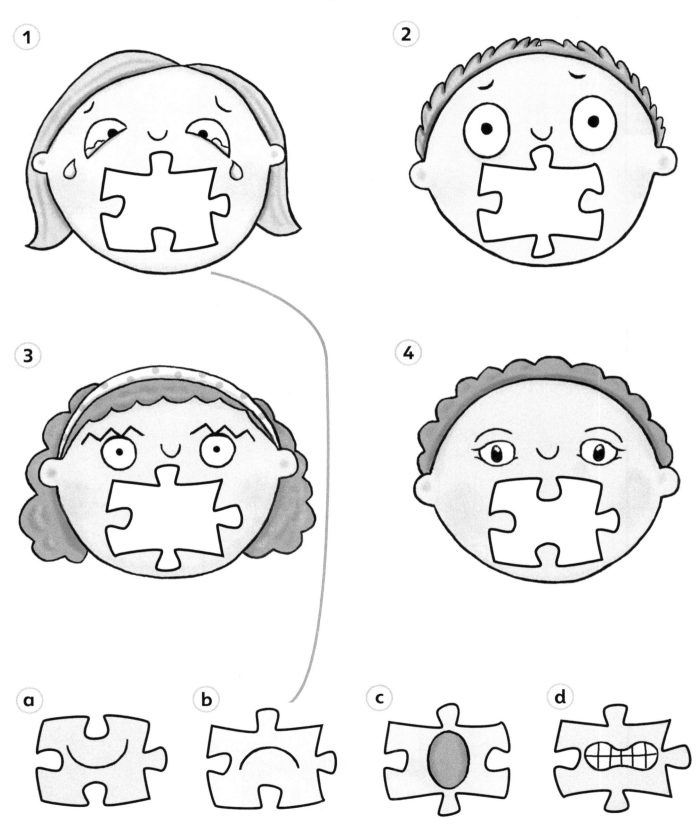

Grammar 1: I'm/You're (angry, happy, sad, scared).

Super Minds Teacher's Resource Book Starter   © Cambridge University Press 2012   **PHOTOCOPIABLE**

Look, say and circle.

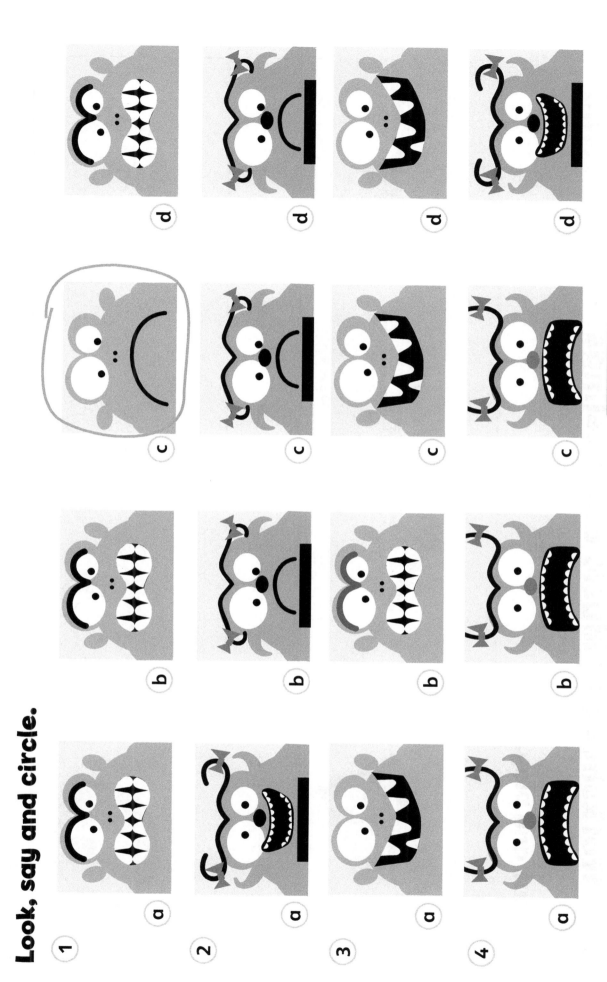

Grammar 2: Are you (angry)? Yes, I am. / No, I'm not.

PHOTOCOPIABLE

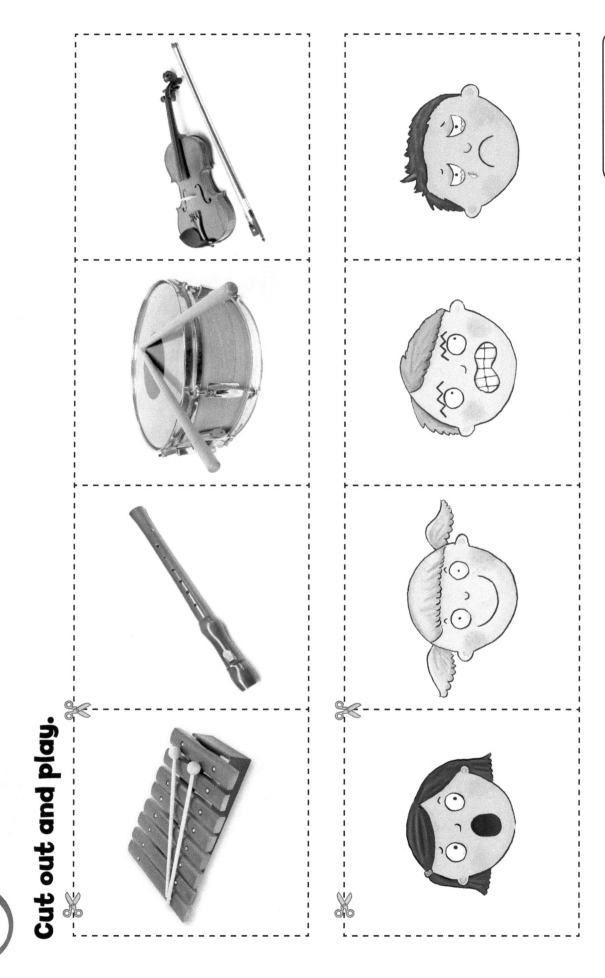

③ Worksheet 4: Music and feelings

Cut out and play.

Super Minds Teacher's Resource Book Starter © Cambridge University Press 2012   **PHOTOCOPIABLE**

4 Toys

Worksheet 1: Toys

Using the worksheet

- This colour by numbers activity practises toy vocabulary *doll, ball, kite, rope, teddy bear, plane* and revises colours *red, yellow, blue, green, purple* and *orange*.

- Students fill in different colours for the paint blobs at the top of the activity to make a personal colour key. They then use this key to colour in the picture beneath.

- Students can then describe their pictures to a partner, e.g. *It's a ball. It's red, green and blue.* They compare what is the same and different about their pictures.

Optional follow-up activity: Play a game of Find something (red). Ask students to find objects in different colours around the classroom. You can either just give a colour instruction, e.g. *Find something red,* for students to point to anything in that colour. Or you can make the instructions specific, e.g. *Find a red pencil. Find a blue book,* etc.

Worksheet 2: I've got a ball.

Using the worksheet

- This maze activity practises the structure *I've got a … and revises toy vocabulary *ball, kite, plane, teddy bear, doll, rope.*

- Students look at the 'Mike' example and follow the path for the other two characters through the maze, using a different colour pencil for each character and circling the three toys they find along the way. They draw these toys in the toy box at the end of each path and colour them. They then say what the character has got, using the first person, e.g. *I'm Mike. I've got a ball. I've got a plane. I've got a teddy bear.*

KEY: I'm Leo. I've got a ball. I've got a kite. I've got a plane. **I'm Polly.** I've got a doll. I've got a kite. I've got a rope.

Optional follow-up activity: Students work in pairs to play a describe and name game. One student chooses a character and describes what they've got in the first person: *I've got a ball. I've got a plane. I've got a teddy bear.* The other student listens and guesses the character they are, e.g. *You're Mike.*

Worksheet 3: Numbers 7 to 10

Using the worksheet

- This matching activity practises numbers 7 to 10 and revises toy vocabulary *ball, doll, rope, teddy bear.*

- Students count out loud the objects in each picture and write the number in the box. Then they draw a line between the pairs of pictures with the same number of the same toy in each. If you check this in class, students can say the letters of the two pictures which are the same and then the number of things that they have counted, e.g. *a and f – ten balls.*

KEY: b,g (eight balls); c,d (six dolls); e,j (seven dolls); h,k (nine ropes); i,l (ten teddy bears)

Optional follow-up activity: Pairs of students cut up the pictures on their worksheets to make sets of cards, then use them to play a game of Matching pairs or Snap! (see page 4).

Worksheet 4: Let's play!

Using the worksheet

- This board game practises actions *hop, skip, jump, throw, catch* and *bounce* and revises toy vocabulary *ball, kite, rope, plane.* It is based on the traditional playground game of Hopscotch (see page 5).

- Students play in pairs using counters and a real or plastic coin. They place their counters on the Start arrow. They then take turns to flip the coin. If the coin lands on heads, they move forward one space. If the coin lands on tails, they move two spaces. If they have landed on a picture of a toy, they say the word and mime playing with it. If it is a picture of an action, they say the action for their partner to act out. The first student to go all the way to square 10 and then back to 1 is the winner.

Optional follow-up activity: Students play Hopscotch in the classroom or playground.

Worksheet 1: Toys

Colour and say.

| 1 | 2 | 3 | 4 | 5 | 6 |

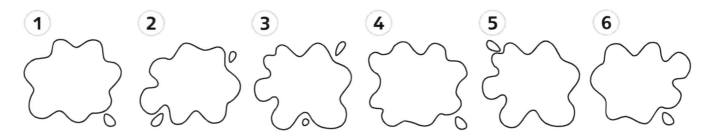

THE TOY SHOP

Vocabulary: ball, kite, rope, teddy bear, doll, plane

Super Minds Teacher's Resource Book Starter   © Cambridge University Press 2012   **PHOTOCOPIABLE**

Find and draw. Then say.

Grammar 1: I've got a (ball).

PHOTOCOPIABLE © Cambridge University Press 2012 *Super Minds* Teacher's Resource Book Starter

Write the numbers and match.

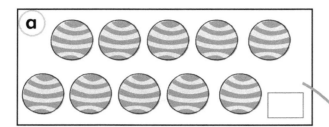

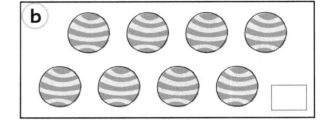

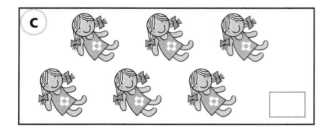

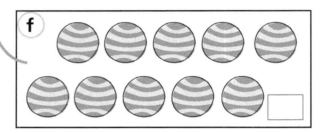

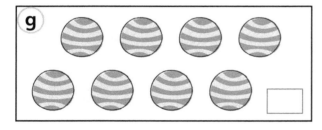

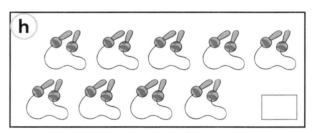

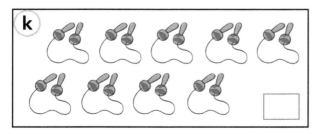

Grammar 2: seven, eight, nine, ten

Super Minds Teacher's Resource Book Starter © Cambridge University Press 2012 **PHOTOCOPIABLE**

Worksheet 4: Let's play!

Play the game.

Let's play Hopscotch!

PHOTOCOPIABLE © Cambridge University Press 2012 *Super Minds* Teacher's Resource Book Starter

5 My house

Worksheet 1: My house

Using the worksheet

- This match and draw activity practises furniture vocabulary *bath*, *bed*, *cupboard*, *table*, *sofa*, *armchair*.

- Students look at the complete furniture pictures round the puzzle picture and say the words. They then match them to the furniture outlines in the puzzle picture, choose a different colour for each and draw round the outlines, filling in any details.

- Students can then compare their pictures in pairs, saying what colours they have used, e.g. *My bath is red*.

Optional follow-up activity: Students play a furniture mime game. Call out items of furniture. They listen and mime an action to do with the furniture item, e.g. mime sleeping for *bed*, washing for *bath*, eating for *table*, sitting for *armchair*, etc.

Worksheet 2: in, on, under

Using the worksheet

- This jigsaw activity practises prepositions *in*, *on*, *under*. It also revises toys *kite*, *ball*, *teddy bear*; classroom objects *book*, *bag* and furniture vocabulary *bed*, *armchair*, *table*, *sofa*, *cupboard*.

- Students say the names of the objects in the jigsaw pieces and draw lines to the correct places in the room picture. They say where these objects are: *in*, *on*, or *under* the furniture in the picture, e.g. **1** *on the bed*.

- Students can then complete the details in the main picture or cut out and stick the jigsaw pieces, then colour the objects in.

KEY: **2** a ball in the cupboard, **3** a book under the sofa, **4** a bag on the table, **5** a teddy bear under the armchair

Optional follow-up activity: Play an instructions game. Ask students to each take a small classroom object, e.g. a pencil. Give instructions, emphasizing the preposition each time, e.g. *Put the pencil under the table. Put the pencil on a chair*, etc. Students follow your instructions. You can also revise other vocabulary areas, e.g. the face: *Put a pencil under your nose*, etc.

Worksheet 3: The doll is on the sofa.

Using the worksheet

- This spot the difference activity practises the structure *The (doll) is (on) the (sofa)*. It also revises toys *doll*, *kite*, *teddy bear*, *plane*, *ball*, furniture vocabulary *sofa*, *armchair*, *cupboard*, *table* and prepositions *in*, *on* and *under*.

- Students look at the two pictures and circle the four other differences. Check by eliciting sentences about the pictures, e.g. *In picture 1, the doll is in the cupboard. In picture 2, the doll is on the sofa*.

- Students can then work in pairs. They take turns to make a sentence about one of the pictures, e.g. *The teddy bear is in the cupboard*. Their partner points to the toy and says the picture number, e.g. *Picture 2!*

- Alternatively, put the class into pairs. Cut the worksheet in half and give each student in the pair one picture. Without looking at their partner's picture, they have to describe their pictures to each other and either circle what's different or draw their partner's toy in the correct place on their picture.

KEY: Pic 1 The ball is under the table/pic 2 on the table; Pic 1 The kite is on the armchair/pic 2 under the table; Pic 1 The teddy bear is under the sofa/pic 2 in the cupboard; Pic 1 The plane is on the table/pic 2 on the cupboard.

Optional follow-up activity: Play a memory game. Put four small objects around the room, e.g. a book on your desk, a rubber under a chair, a bag on a chair, a pencil in a cupboard. Ask students to remember where these objects are. Then ask them to close their eyes. Move one of the objects to a different location, e.g. put the book under your desk. Students then open their eyes. They have to tell you what's different.

Worksheet 4: Homes

Using the worksheet

- This matching activity revises furniture vocabulary *bath*, *bed*, *table*, *sofa*, *cupboard* and practises vocabulary for homes *palace*, *tent*, *tree house* and the structure *The (bed) is in the (palace)*. It encourages students to compare furniture in different types of dwelling.

- Students decide which dwelling is most appropriate for each type of furniture and draw lines to match them up. Check by eliciting sentences, e.g. *1 The bath is in the palace*.

- They then decide which place they would like to live in.

KEY: **2** The bath is in the tree house. **3** The bed is in the tent. **4** The bed is in the palace. **5** The bed is in the tree house. **6** The table is in the tent. **7** The table is in the palace. **8** The sofa is in the palace. **9** The cupboard is in the tree house. **10** The cupboard is in the palace.

Optional follow-up activity: Students design their own furniture for an unusual home they would like to live in.

Worksheet 1: My house

Say, match and draw.

bed

bath

cupboard

table

sofa

armchair

Vocabulary: bath, bed, cupboard, table, sofa, armchair

PHOTOCOPIABLE

Say. Then match and draw.

Grammar 1: in, on, under

5 Worksheet 3: The doll is on the sofa.

Find and circle. Then say.

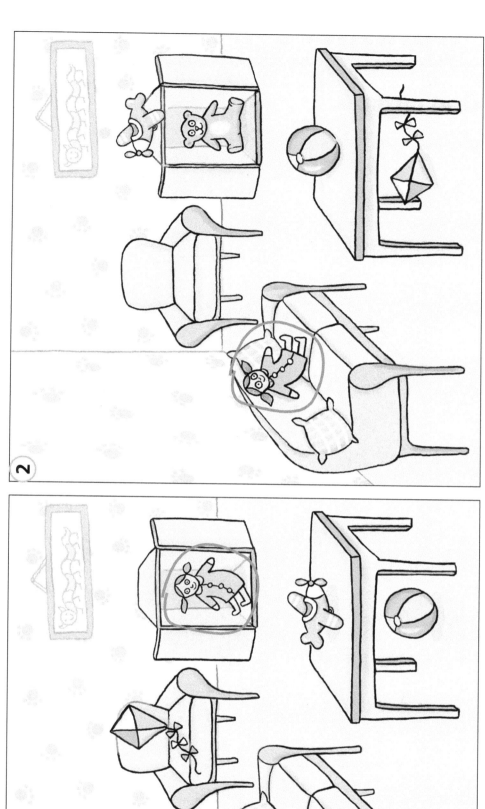

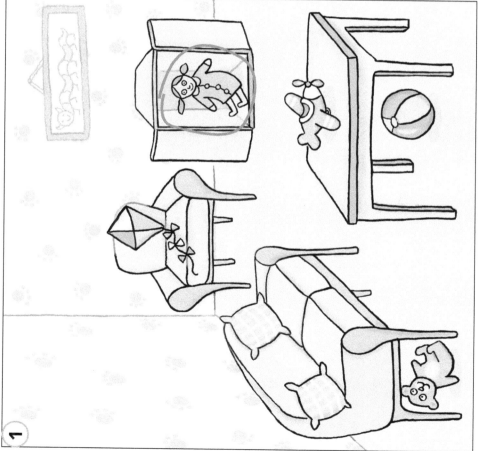

Grammar 2: The (doll) is (on) the (sofa).

PHOTOCOPIABLE © Cambridge University Press 2012   *Super Minds* Teacher's Resource Book Starter

Worksheet 4: Homes

Look and match.

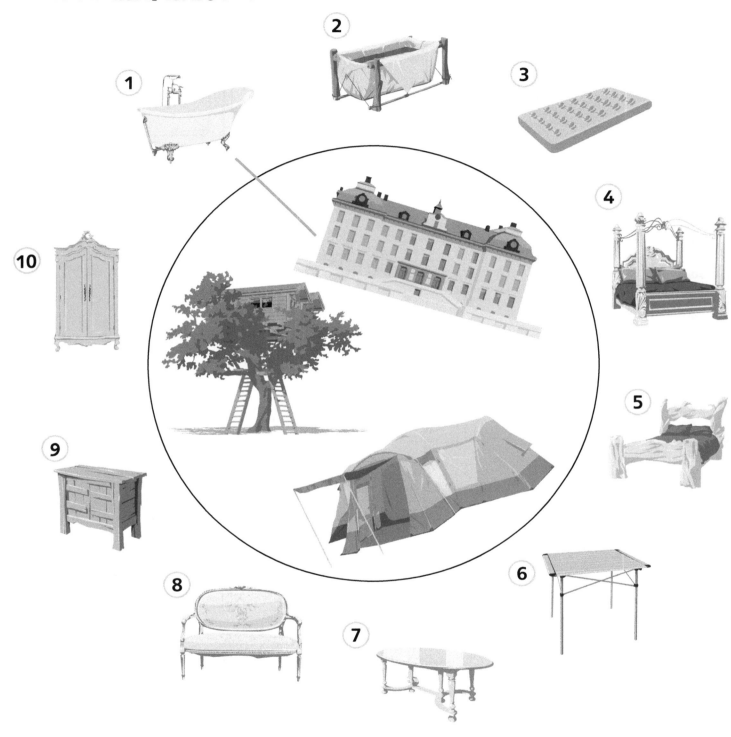

6 On the farm

Worksheet 1: Animals on the farm

Using the worksheet

- This matching activity practises animal vocabulary *cat*, *dog*, *horse*, *rabbit*, *cow*, *sheep*.

- Students match the two parts of each animal by drawing a line. They say the correct animal word as they do so.

- Students can then work in pairs. They take turns to say the name of an animal for their partner to point to the correct face.

KEY: **2**f cow, **3**b dog, **4**e horse, **5**d rabbit, **6**a sheep

Optional follow-up activity: Students cut out the half pictures and put them together to make the complete animals. They can also put them together in different combinations, e.g. the front half of the cat with the back half of the dog. Encourage them to name these combinations, e.g. *a cat-dog!*

Worksheet 2: I like cats.

Using the worksheet

- This maze activity practises the structure *I like …* and revises animal vocabulary *cat*, *rabbit*, *horse*, *cow*, *dog*, *sheep* and their plurals.

- Students follow the path for the boy and girl monsters through the maze and circle the three animals they find along the way. These are the animals that the monsters like.

- They then tick the animals that each monster likes in the thought bubble at the bottom of the page. Check the activity by asking students to say what each monster likes, using the first person, e.g. *I'm monster 1. I like cats*. Make sure they use the plural form of the animals in their sentences.

KEY: **1** I like cows. I like dogs. I like sheep. **2** I like rabbits. I like horses. I like cats.

Optional follow-up activity: Students work in small groups to play a guessing game. Each student draws two or three animals they like onto one piece of paper. These are then folded up and put into a pile on the table. Students take it in turns to pick up a piece of paper from the table and make sentences using the animal names, e.g. *I like cats. I like dogs*. The others have to guess the name of the student who drew these animals.

Worksheet 3: My favourite

Using the worksheet

- This puzzle activity practises the structure *My favourite … is / are …* and revises toy vocabulary *ball*, *teddy bear*, *plane*, *kite* and colours.

- Choosing a different colour for each character, students colour the shapes with dots in them in each picture puzzle to find out what that character's favourite toy is.

- Students can then work in pairs. Using the first person, they describe each character's favourite toy, e.g. *I'm Mike. My favourite toys are balls* and favourite colour, e.g. *My favourite colour is red*, according to which colour they have chosen.

KEY: **2** I'm Polly. My favourite toys are teddy bears. **3** I'm Leo. My favourite toys are planes. **4** I'm Gina. My favourite toys are kites.

Optional follow-up activity: Students design their own picture puzzle for others in the class to colour in and find out their favourite toy. Alternatively, they can do a similar picture puzzle of an animal instead.

Worksheet 4: Animal homes

Using the worksheet

- This Bingo game practises animal vocabulary *cow*, *horse*, *sheep*, *shark*, *dolphin*, *whale*, *lion*, *giraffe*, *elephant*, *parrot*, *snake*, *monkey*, animal habitats *the sea*, *the savannah*, *a farm* and the structure, *(Giraffes) live (in the savannah)*.

- Encourage students to name the animals they can see on the worksheet first. Help them as necessary.

- Students each choose a card and use it to play a game of Bingo. Point out the three different habitats in column 1, *the savannah*, *a farm*, *the sea*. To play the game, say sentences randomly about each of the animals on the worksheet and where they live, e.g. *A farm. Horses live on a farm. / The sea. Sharks live in the sea. / The savannah. Elephants live in the savannah*. Students listen and cross out the animals on the card they have chosen as you say them. When they have crossed them all out, they put up their hand and call out *Bingo!* The first student to do this is the winner, even if other students have also just completed their cards.

Optional follow-up activity: Play an animal mime game. Call out one of the animal habitats, e.g. *savannah*. Students have to mime one of the animals that live there. Others in the class guess what each student is miming.

Worksheet 1: Animals on the farm

Match and say.

1 cat	a
2 cow	b
3 dog	c
4 horse	d
5 rabbit	e
6 sheep	f

Vocabulary: cat, horse, cow, dog, rabbit, sheep

Super Minds Teacher's Resource Book Starter   © Cambridge University Press 2012   **PHOTOCOPIABLE**

Follow and circle. Then tick (✓).

Grammar 1: I like (cats).

PHOTOCOPIABLE   © Cambridge University Press 2012   *Super Minds* Teacher's Resource Book Starter

Colour and say.

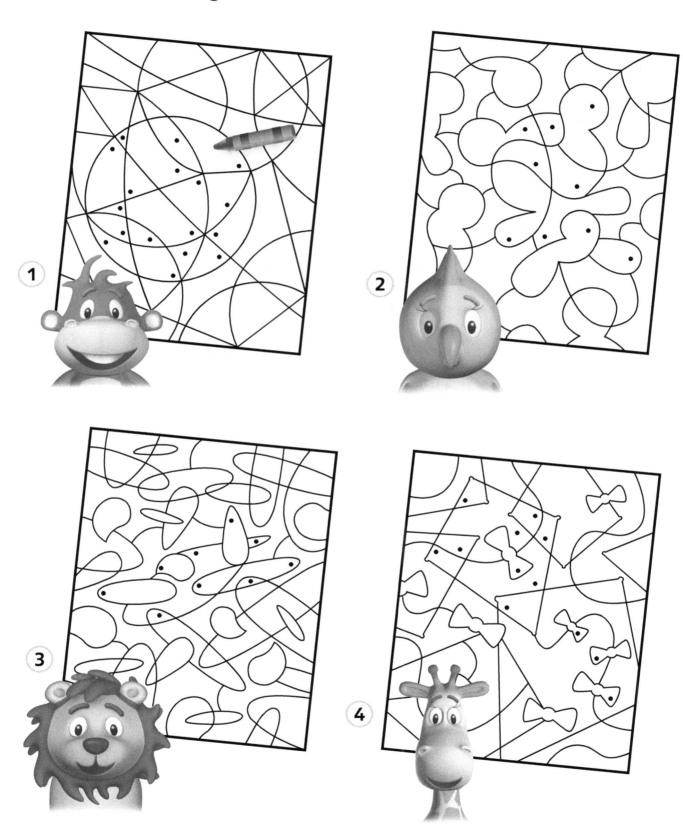

Grammar 2: My favourite colour is (blue) / toys are (planes).

Super Minds Teacher's Resource Book Starter © Cambridge University Press 2012 **PHOTOCOPIABLE**

Play animal bingo.

1

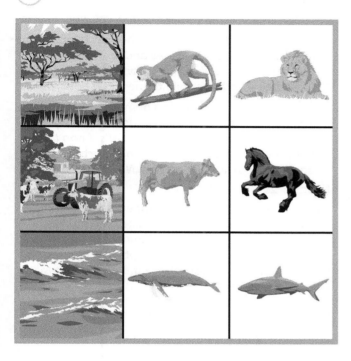

2

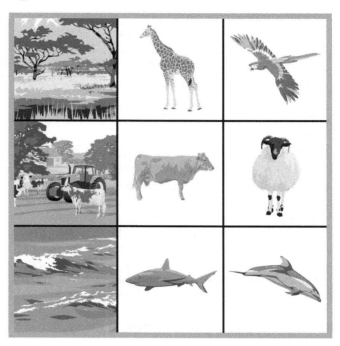

3

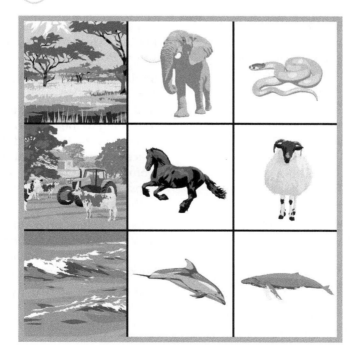

Animal homes

7 I'm hungry!

Worksheet 1: Food

Using the worksheet

- This spot the difference activity practises food vocabulary *carrots*, *sausages*, *apples*, *cakes*, *ice cream*, *chips* and revises numbers 1 to 10.

- Students count the different foods and find the differences between the two pictures. They circle the additional food in picture 2.

- Check by asking *How many …* questions, e.g. *Look at picture 1. How many carrots?*

KEY: Pic 1 four sausages/pic 2 six sausages; Pic 1 two apples/pic 2 three apples; Pic 1 seven cakes/pic 2 nine cakes; Pic 1 one ice cream/pic 2 two ice creams; Pic 1 nine chips/pic 2 ten chips

Optional follow-up activity: Play a memory game, using a tray or table with different numbers of plastic food items or pictures, e.g. two apples, three cakes. Students look at the food for a minute, then shut their eyes while you change something (add another apple, take away a cake, etc.). Students open their eyes and tell you what is different, e.g. *Three apples!* You could play this game with e.g. rubbers, pencils, etc.

Worksheet 2: I like … I don't like …

Using the worksheet

- This observation activity practises *I like … / I don't like …* and revises food vocabulary *carrots*, *sausages*, *apples*, *cakes*, *ice cream*, *chips*.

- Students tell you the names of the food items in the grid. Then demonstrate the activity. Students look at the pictures of the four children at the top of the page and tick in the grid the food that each child likes. Encourage them to say, in the first person, what each child likes and doesn't like, e.g. *I like sausages, chips and cakes. I don't like carrots, apples and ice cream.*

KEY: **2** I like carrots, chips and apples. I don't like sausages, cakes and ice cream. **3** I like cakes, apples and ice cream. I don't like sausages, carrots and chips. **4** I like sausages, carrots and ice cream. I don't like chips, apples and cakes.

Optional follow-up activity: Stick or draw pictures in a horizontal line on the board of the food *carrots*, *sausages*, *apples*, *cakes*, *ice cream* and *chips*. Put a tick at the start of the line to show *I like …* . Repeat the pictures with a cross at the other side of the board to show *I don't like …* . Students line up in three teams. Say a sentence, e.g. *I don't like ice cream*. The first student from the front of a team to run and touch the correct picture gets a point.

Worksheet 3: I like … I don't like …

Using the worksheet

- This matching activity practises the structures *I like … / I don't like …* and revises toy and animal vocabulary *doll*, *teddy bear*, *plane*, *cat*, *dog*, *rabbit*.

- Students look at the children's thought bubbles and describe what each one likes and doesn't like in the first person, e.g. *I like dolls. I don't like teddy bears.* They then match the child to the correct bedroom.

- This can also be played as a game in pairs. Students secretly choose one of the characters and say what they do and don't like, e.g. *I like dolls. I don't like teddy bears. I like planes*, etc. Their partner listens and guesses who they are, e.g. *Number 1!*

KEY: 1c, 2a, 3b

Optional follow-up activity: Students play a game of *True or False* about their own likes and dislikes. In pairs, they take turns to say sentences about toys, animals, colours or food for their partner to guess whether they are true or false, e.g. *I like sausages. I don't like ice cream.*

Worksheet 4: Our food

Using the worksheet

- This board game practises the structure (*Eggs*) *come from* (*hens*); food vocabulary *apples*, *carrots*, *eggs* and *milk* and places that food comes from *trees*, *the ground*, *hens*, *cows*.

- Tell students they are going to a farm to collect some food. Elicit the names of the food in the baskets, which they have to collect, and where food comes from.

- Students work in pairs. Each one chooses one of the baskets. They put their counters on number 1 and take turns to throw a dice or spin a spinner. According to the number, students push their counter round the board. They say the name of the place where they land and the food that comes from it, e.g. *hen – eggs*, or make a sentence, e.g. *Eggs come from hens.* They then tick off that food in their basket.

- When they land on a place they have already ticked, they do nothing, travelling round the board until one student has collected all the food for their basket. This student is the winner.

Optional follow-up activity: If you have the facilities, try growing some carrots or other simple vegetables in pots or outside.

7 Worksheet 1: Food

Find and circle.

1

cakes   ice cream   carrots

chips   sausages   apples

2

Vocabulary: carrots, sausages, apples, cakes, ice cream, chips

Look and tick (✓).

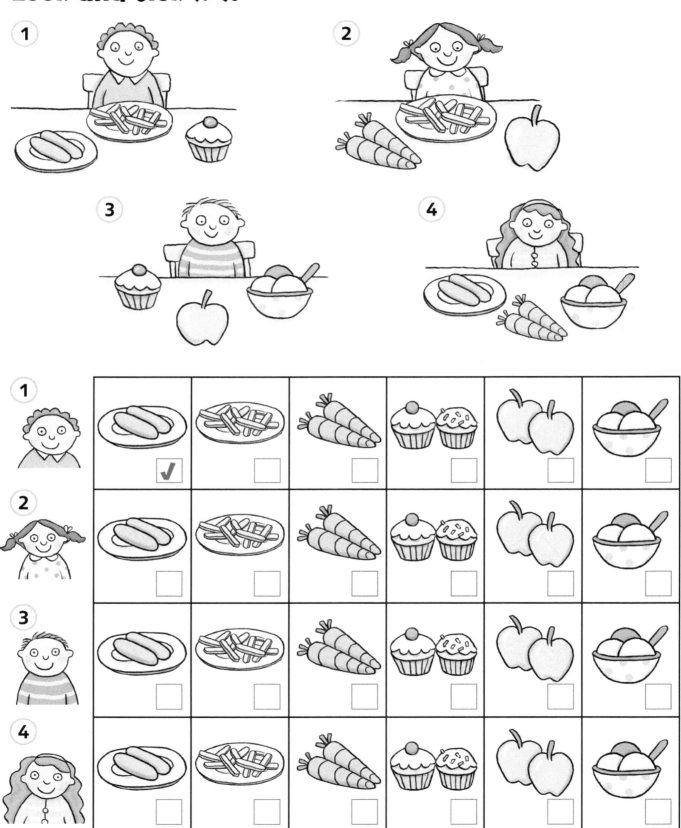

Grammar 1: I like / I don't like (carrots).

7 **Worksheet 3: I like … I don't like …**

Look and say. Then match.

1

2

3

a

b

c

Grammar 2: I like / I don't like (blue, cats, dolls).

PHOTOCOPIABLE © Cambridge University Press 2012   *Super Minds* Teacher's Resource Book Starter

Play the game.

Our food

8 All aboard!

Worksheet 1: Transport

Using the worksheet

- This matching activity practises transport vocabulary *car, train, boat, bike, scooter, bus*.

- Students find and match the partial views in the circles with the correct transport item by drawing a line. They say the transport words.

KEY: 2d scooter, 3b train, 4e bus, 5a boat, 6f car

Optional follow-up activity: The class play a transport mime game. Ask for volunteers to mime transport by riding or driving the items you whisper to them. The other students have to say what type of transport it is. Alternatively, students can play in pairs, using the worksheet. One student mimes a transport item, their partner points to the picture and says the word.

Worksheet 2: I'm driving.

Using the worksheet

- This observation activity practises the structure *I'm ... -ing* and the verbs *riding, sailing, driving, flying* and revises transport vocabulary *car, train, boat, bike, plane, bus*.

- Students look at the children at the top of the page. They find them in the main picture, draw a line to match them and then say what they are doing, using the first person, e.g. *Number 1 I'm riding (a bike)*. Students can either use the verb only or add the correct transport item to the sentence as well, depending on their level.

KEY: 2 I'm sailing (a boat). 3 I'm driving (a bus).
4 I'm driving (a car). 5 I'm driving (a train).
6 I'm flying (a plane).

Optional follow-up activity: Play Chinese whispers. Students stand in lines of about six. Whisper the same sentence to the first student in each line, e.g. *I'm driving a train*. Students pass the whisper down the line. Each student can only say the sentence once so must be very clear. The last student in the line must listen, then do the action. The team get a point if they have successfully passed on the whisper. Repeat with a new instruction or with different instructions to each team.

Worksheet 3: climbing, flying, running

Using the worksheet

- This noughts and crosses game practises *I'm climbing a tree, swimming, flying a kite, running, brushing my teeth, washing my hands, driving a car, sailing a boat, riding a bike*.

- Students look at the grid first and make sentences for each of the pictures.

- Students then play in pairs: one is noughts; one is crosses. One student starts by choosing a space on the grid and making a sentence about it, e.g. *I'm riding a bike*. If the sentence is correct, they put their nought (O) or cross in the box next to that picture. If the sentence is incorrect, they put nothing. Their partner then has a turn. The game continues until one student has put three noughts or three crosses in a horizontal, vertical or diagonal line. They are the winner.

- Note that if students use pencil, they can play the game several times. Note also that students can play in groups of three with one student acting as an adjudicator on correct and incorrect sentences.

KEY: 1 I'm climbing a tree. 2 I'm swimming.
3 I'm flying a kite. 4 I'm running. 5 I'm brushing my teeth. 6 I'm washing my hands. 7 I'm driving a car. 8 I'm sailing a boat. 9 I'm riding a bike.

Optional follow-up activity: Students can cut up the pictures to make a set of cards for Matching pairs or Snap! (see page 4).

Worksheet 4: Shapes

Using the worksheet

- This dice-based colouring game revises shapes *rectangle, square, triangle, circle*; colours *red, blue, green, orange, purple, yellow*; forms of transport *car, train, boat, bus* and numbers up to six.

- Students can work in small groups of up to four. Each group will need access to coloured pencils and a dice or spinner to play the game. You can decide with the class what colour each number will be, e.g. 1 = blue, or leave it to each child to choose.

- Each student chooses a shapes picture to complete. They take it in turns to shake the dice or spin the spinner and colour the appropriate numbers on their picture. If they throw or spin a number they have already coloured in, they do nothing. The first student to colour in their whole picture is the winner.

- Encourage students to name the shapes and the colours they are using as they play the game, e.g. *1 – a triangle. Red!* When students have finished their pictures, they can describe the shapes and colours of their transport, e.g. *A boat. A red triangle, a blue square, an orange triangle*, etc.

Optional follow-up activity: Children cut out shapes from different-coloured paper or card and use these to create shapes pictures of their own.

Match and say.

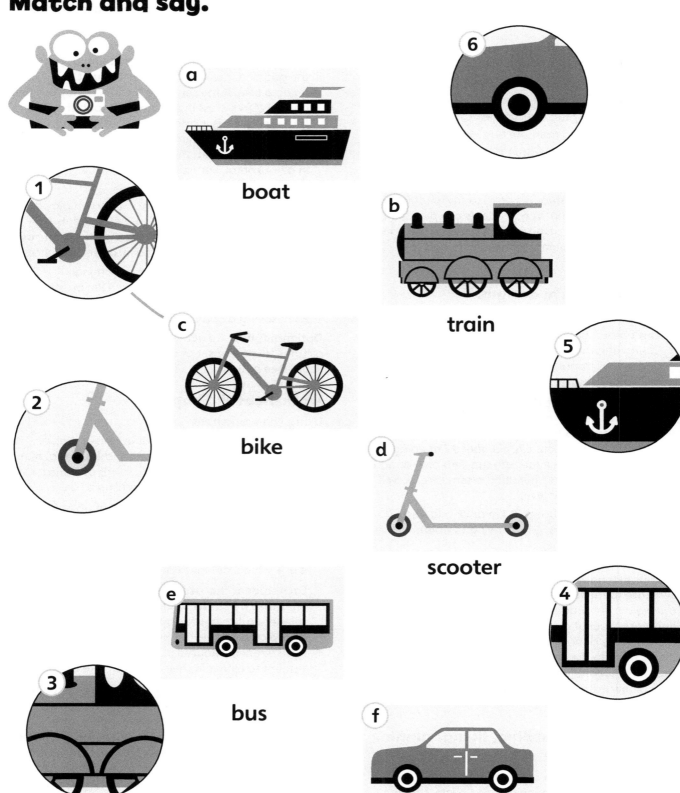

boat

train

bike

scooter

bus

car

Vocabulary: boat, train, car, bike, scooter, bus

8 Worksheet 2: I'm driving.

Find, match and say.

1 2 3 4 5 6

Grammar 1: I'm driving / flying / riding / sailing

PHOTOCOPIABLE © Cambridge University Press 2012   *Super Minds* Teacher's Resource Book Starter

Look and say.
Then play noughts and crosses.

> Grammar 2: flying a kite, swimming, climbing a tree, running, brushing my teeth, washing my hands, …

Play and colour.

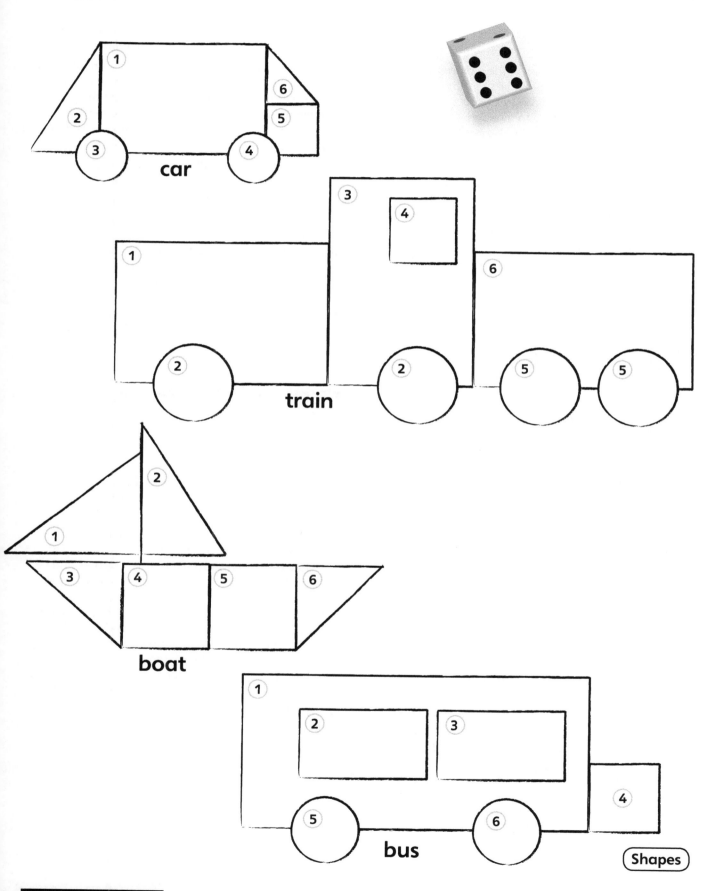

car

train

boat

bus

Shapes

9 Party clothes

Worksheet 1: Clothes

Using the worksheet

- This match and draw activity practises clothes vocabulary *hat*, *shirt*, *boots*, *shoes*, *belt*, *badge*.

- Students draw a line to match the pictures of the clothes to the dotted outlines of the same items on the bed. They then trace round the dotted outlines and add any other details to make the pairs of pictures match completely. They then read out the clothes labels.

- Students can then use the two sets of clothes for a pairwork information-gap activity. One student colours in the clothes on the washing line and the other colours the clothes on the bed. They then describe the colours they have chosen to their partner, e.g. *a red shirt*. Their partner listens and uses the same colours to colour in the appropriate clothes on their own worksheet.

KEY: 2f, 3c, 4b, 5a, 6e

Optional follow-up activity: With the whole class, call out clothes items and ask students to mime putting them on. Or ask students to play *What are the clothes?* in pairs, using the worksheet: one student mimes putting on a clothes item, the other points to it on the worksheet and says the word.

Worksheet 2: I like ...

Using the worksheet

- This observation activity revises the structure *I like ...* and food vocabulary *cakes*, *biscuits*, *apples*, *carrots*, *chips*, *crisps*, *sweets*, *salad*, *ice cream*, *sausages*.

- Students note the food items the monsters are eating and then find and circle them in the appropriate row in the grid. They should say *I like* and the correct food item, e.g. *I like biscuits* each time. Encourage students to say what they don't like too, e.g. *I don't like cakes. I don't like crisps. I don't like sweets.*

- Students can then work in pairs. One chooses a monster and makes a sentence about what they like, e.g. *I like salad.* Their partner listens and guesses who they are, e.g. *Number 2!*

KEY: 2 salad, 3 cakes, 4 crisps, 5 sweets, 6 ice cream

Optional follow-up activity: Play a game of *I agree*. Make statements about things you like, e.g. *I like ice cream.* All students who agree with you stand up and mime eating an ice cream. Those who don't like ice cream stay sitting down and then say *I don't like ice cream.* Repeat with other foods or words that students know in English. For animals or toys they can mime being the animal or playing with the toy.

Worksheet 3: I've got ...

Using the worksheet

- This follow the path activity revises *I've got ...* and the vocabulary *rabbit*, *car*, *boat* and *book*.

- Students draw over the tangled lines with different colours to discover which present each character on the worksheet has. They then complete the picture of the present and say what the character has got, using the first person, e.g. *I'm Polly. I've got a rabbit.*

- Students can then work in pairs. One makes a sentence, e.g. *I've got a rabbit.* The other says what character they are, e.g. *You're Polly.*

KEY: 2c I'm Leo. I've got a car. 3a I'm Gina. I've got a boat. 4b I'm Mike. I've got a book.

Optional follow-up activity: Students do an information-gap activity. They each draw outlines of two present boxes, one above the other, on a piece of paper and then secretly draw three items inside the top one. They then work in pairs and say what presents they've got. Their partner listens and draws them into the bottom box on their paper before comparing.

Worksheet 4: Party clothes

Using the worksheet

- This activity practises the structure *I've got ...* and the vocabulary *hat*, *crown*, *shirt*, *boots*, *shoes*, *badge*, *belt*, *nose*, *bag*.

- Students look at the pictures of the different characters and name the clothes they can see on the cards next to them.

- Students then cut out the pictures to make a card game. In groups of four, they each choose a character, then shuffle the other pictures and spread them out face down between them. They take turns to turn a picture face up. If it belongs to the character they are collecting, they say what they've got, e.g. *I've got a crown*, and keep the card. If it doesn't belong to their character, they name the item but replace the picture face down in the same place. The winner is the first student to collect all four pieces belonging to their character.

Optional follow-up activity: Students draw the completed characters and colour them in.

Worksheet 1: Clothes

Match, draw and say.

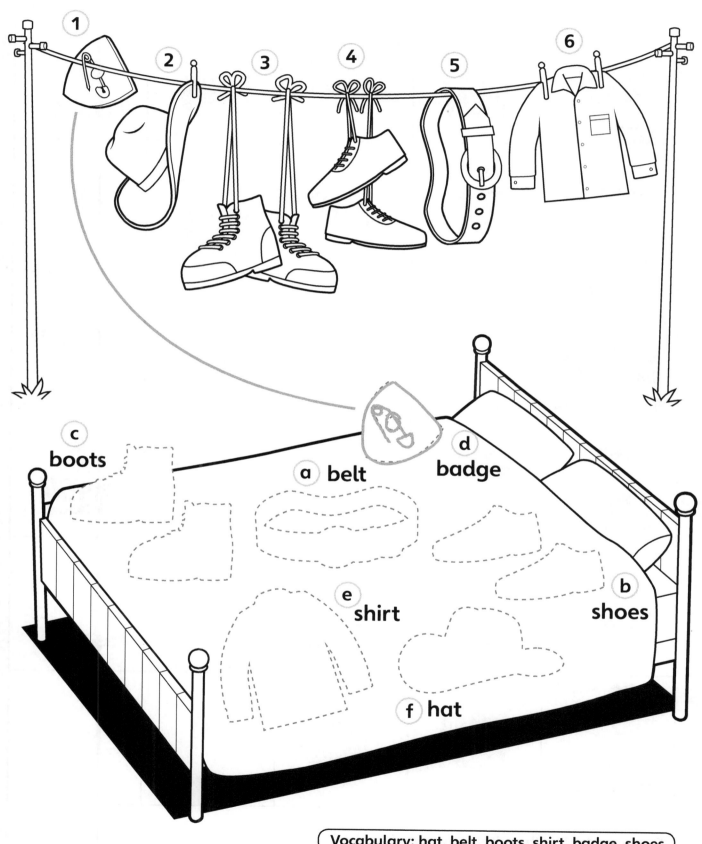

Vocabulary: hat, belt, boots, shirt, badge, shoes

PHOTOCOPIABLE © Cambridge University Press 2012 *Super Minds* Teacher's Resource Book Starter

Worksheet 2: I like ...

Find, circle and say.

Grammar 1: I like (biscuits, crisps, salad, sweets).

9 Worksheet 3: I've got ...

Match and complete. Then say.

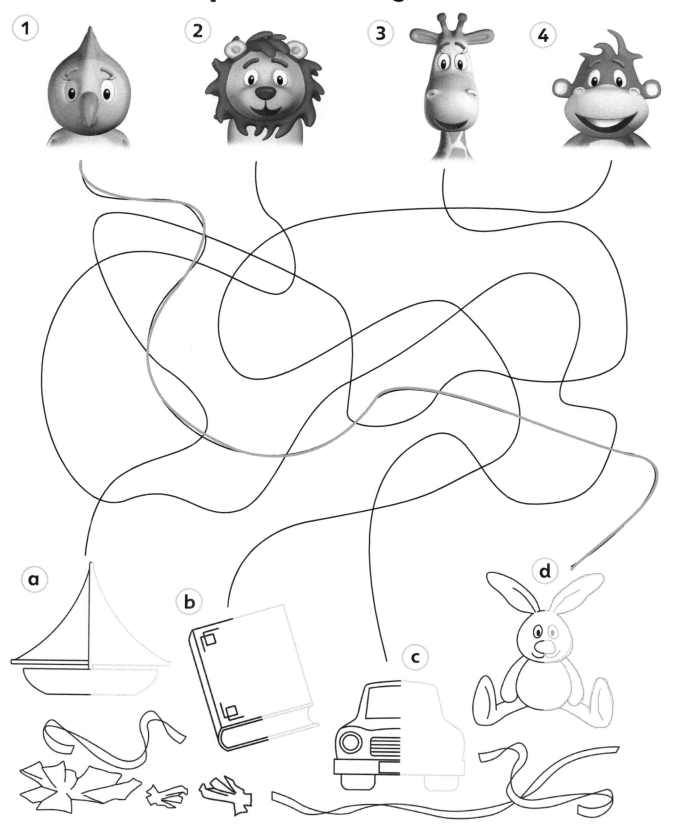

Grammar 2: I've got (a ball).

PHOTOCOPIABLE © Cambridge University Press 2012 *Super Minds* Teacher's Resource Book Starter

Worksheet 4: Party clothes

Say, cut and play.

Clothes

Super Minds Teacher's Resource Book Starter   © Cambridge University Press 2012   **PHOTOCOPIABLE**

Acknowledgements

The publishers are grateful to the following illustrators:
Bill Bolton; Martin Lowe; Marek Jagucki; Theresa Tibbetts (Beehive);
Martin Sanders (Beehive); Kate Daubney

The publishers are grateful to the following contributors:
Lynne Rushton: freelance editor
Oliver Design: concept design
Pentacor**big**: cover design, book design and page make-up

Lightning Source UK Ltd.
Milton Keynes UK
UKHW050958250822
407703UK00002B/15

9 781107 640139